Let's Share

By Janine Amos and Annabel Spenceley

Consultant Rachael Underwood

an imprint of
WINDMILL BOOKS ™
New York

Published in the United States by Alphabet Soup, an imprint of Windmill Books, LLC

Windmill Books
303 Park Avenue South
Suite #1280
New York, NY 10010

U.S. publication copyright © 2010 Evans Brothers Limited
First North American Edition

Library of Congress Cataloging-in-Publication Data

Amos, Janine
     Let's share. – 1st North American ed. / by Janine Amos and Annabel Spenceley.
cm. – (Best behavior)
     Contents: Playing with clay—Strawberries!
     Summary: Two brief stories demonstrate the importance of working things out fairly when two people want the same thing.
     ISBN 978-1-60754-508-8 (lib.) – 978-1-60754-509-5 (pbk.)
978-1-60754-511-8 (6 pack)
     1. Sharing—Juvenile literature   [1. Sharing   2. Conduct of life]
I. Spenceley, Annabel   II. Title   III. Series
     177/.1—dc22

Manufactured in China

With thanks to: Holly Benham, Lewis Jamieson, Chaitun Bagary, Megan and Maya Sear.

Playing with Clay

Lewis is playing with all the modeling clay.

Holly wants to play too.

Holly grabs the clay.

Lewis yells.
How does he feel?

Louise comes to
talk to them.

"What's going on?" she asks.

9

"I want the clay!"
shouts Holly.

"I was using it!" screams Lewis.

"Lewis, you sound angry,"
says Louise.

"And, Holly, you really want
the clay."

Holly and Lewis nod.

"I need lots of clay to make animals," says Lewis.

"I need some to make a pizza," says Holly.

16

Holly and Lewis both
want the clay.
What could they do?

Holly thinks hard.

"Lewis can give me some of the clay to make my pizza," she says. "He can have the rest."

19

Lewis thinks about it.

He gives Holly one handful of clay. Then he gives her some more.

"You've solved the problem. You are sharing the clay," says Louise.

Strawberries!

Maya has some strawberries.

Megan comes over.
"I want some, too," she says.

"Here," says Maya.

Megan takes lots of strawberries.
"Hey!" says Maya. "That's too many!"

Megan looks at the strawberries.
"I know!" she says.

What do you think Megan will do?

Megan gives
some of the
strawberries
back to Maya.

Now they each
have half.

FOR FURTHER READING

INFORMATION BOOKS
Llewellyn, Claire. *Why Should I Share?* Hauppauge, NY: Barron's Educational Series, 2005.

Meiners, Cheri J. *Share and Take Turns*. Minneapolis: Free Spirit Publishing, 2003.

FICTION
Munsch, Robert N. *We Share Everything*. New York: Cartwheel Books, 2002.

Reiss, Mike. *The Boy Who Wouldn't Share*. New York: HarperCollins, 2008.

AUTHOR BIO

Janine Amos has worked in publishing as an editor and author, and as a lecturer in education. Her interests are in personal growth and raising self-esteem, and she works with educators, child psychologists, and specialists in mediation. She has written more than fifty books for children. Many of her titles deal with first-time experiences and emotional health issues such as bullying, death, and divorce.

You can find more great fiction and nonfiction from Windmill Books at windmillbooks.com